God
Wants
You to
Know...

Ruth L. Coffing

ISBN 978-1-63903-537-3 (paperback)
ISBN 978-1-63903-538-0 (digital)

Copyright © 2022 by Ruth L. Coffing

All rights reserved. No part of this publication may be reproduced, distributed, or transmitted in any form or by any means, including photocopying, recording, or other electronic or mechanical methods without the prior written permission of the publisher. For permission requests, solicit the publisher via the address below.

Christian Faith Publishing
832 Park Avenue
Meadville, PA 16335
www.christianfaithpublishing.com

Printed in the United States of America

To God:
*The author and finisher of my faith
and this book.
Selah.*

To my dear friend Ruth,

A simple act of stepping out in faith to obey God has led you on an incredible journey. Thank you for sharing the words He has given you. What started out as writing down what God told you each day turned into something far beyond what you ever expected. I hope and pray the messages inspire the readers of your book to draw closer to God the same way they have me.

Dr. Kelly Meyer

Preface

In obedience, in January 2021, I set aside ten minutes to "be still and know I am God" every day. Following that time, I spent five minutes listening to God. I then wrote down what God spoke to me. I now believe that He was not just speaking to me but to you, the reader, also. I pray that these words will bless you as they have me, that they will encourage and enlighten everyone that reads them. God bless you.

God Wants You to Know...

"I am the Light. No darkness is in Me. Let Me shine on your future. Let Me light up your way everlasting. Come to Me, and soak in My light.

"Your enemies were strong and pompous and victorious, and you were arrogant and defeated. Repent, and ask for forgiveness, and I will send My thunder of victory, the thunder of victory, over your enemies, i.e., complacency, laziness, self-indulgence, settling for less, and disobedience. When you repent, you will have My forgiveness and My favor and My heart, and I will win your battles for you! Amen!"

You need to repent, be sorry for your sins (complacency, laziness, self-indulgence, settling for less, and disobedience), and cry out for God's forgiveness. When you do these things, you will see the victory; things will never be the same.

God

God, I want you to know...

God Wants You to Know…

When we are tired, He relieves us.

Take a break. Stop trying to be everything in your own power. Let Me relieve you from all responsibility for doing and being all things to all people. That is My job, not yours. Give every day over to your helper, the Holy Spirit. When you give Him complete control of your day, you will not get tired. You will soar and have enough energy to do all I ask you to do. I relieve you from all earthly demands on your life and empower you to live out the godly vision I have for you. Selah.

Take each step with a leap of faith. Know that I am with you always. I will not leave you nor forsake you. I know the plans I have for you, plans for peace and well-being and not for disaster, to give you a future and a hope. With Me you can do all things; nothing is impossible. Remember: a goal is a God-ordained activity of love.

Go for it. We got this!

Abba Father

God, I want you to know...

God Wants You to Know...

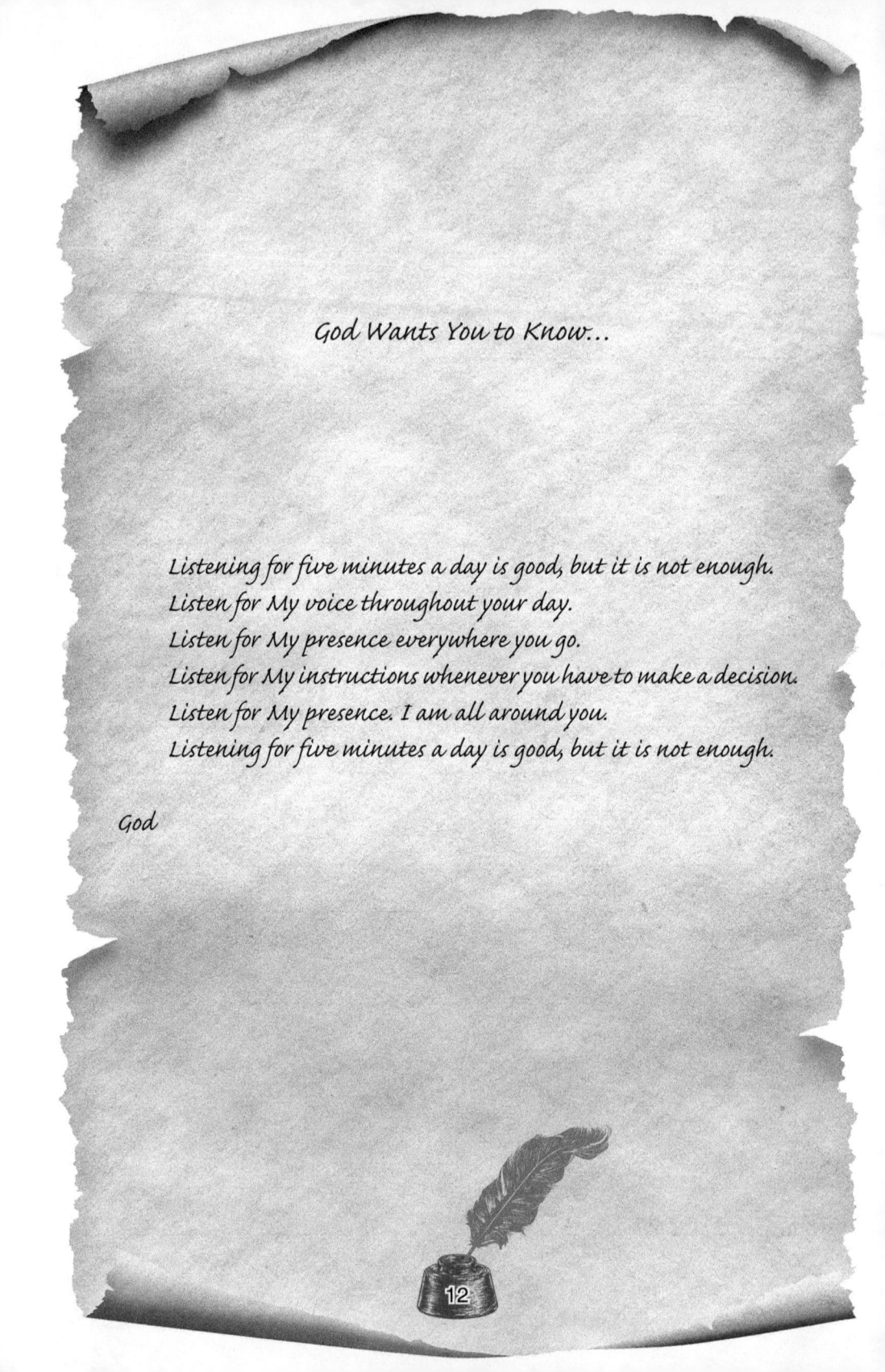

Listening for five minutes a day is good, but it is not enough.
Listen for My voice throughout your day.
Listen for My presence everywhere you go.
Listen for My instructions whenever you have to make a decision.
Listen for My presence. I am all around you.
Listening for five minutes a day is good, but it is not enough.

God

God, I want you to know...

God Wants You to Know...

On your journey, there will be many choices to be made, many decisions to be made, and many discernments to be determined. The quality of your life will be determined by the choices you make. The things you decide to do or not to do and your willingness to allow Me to help you discern every situation, every thought, and every action you make.

Decide to follow Me, to want what I want, and to listen and obey.

Never allow Satan to influence your decisions. Never listen to his persuasive arguments. Never, never, never believe his lies!

When you take what I tell you to heart, you will do the good works I have planned for you to do.

Life is like a puzzle. All the pieces need to be put together before you can see the big picture. You will feel like jamming the pieces together to make them fit, but there is only one way they will fit and that is My way, the way I planned. Work on the part of the puzzle I give you until it is finished, then move on to another part. The end result (the picture of your life) will be worth it.

Trust in Me, and I will show you what you will need to do and when to do it so you will have a beautiful life in Me. Selah.

God

God, I want you to know...

God Wants You to Know...

Do your routine every day, and I will meet you there.

My plan for you is simple but profound. It is easy but challenging. The dream I will put in your heart is the same dream I have in My heart for you. Don't overthink it; accept it. Don't worry or be anxious. Be calm and accepting. Rely on Me for wisdom, the wisdom to make the right decisions and the wisdom to trust My timing. Don't get ahead of Me. Lean not on your own understanding, but lean on me!

Be diligent, be determined, and be disciplined.

Work on what I have given you thus far, and I will promote you when the timing—my timing—is right.

Right now just dream: do your routine every day, and I will meet you there.

God

God, I want you to know...

God Wants You to Know...

    Fear not! To fear is a decision. Decide to fear not. I feel you are afraid of failure and even more fearful of success. You are afraid of doing the wrong thing but also of not doing the right thing.

    Rest (resist every sinful tension) in Me. Resist every sinful tension. Satan is behind stress, worry, fear, and restlessness. Resist the devil, and he will flee! He no longer has power over you! You are free, you are in Me, and I am in you. We are victorious.

    Your future is decided by the decisions you make. Decide to make the right choices. Choose love, light, and freedom. Choose Me every day, in every way, and you will be prosperous, and I will be very proud of you. I love you.

Abba Father,
Daddy God

God, I want you to know...

God Wants You to Know...

    Trust Me and I will trust you to obey. Obey Me and I will trust you even more. This is not difficult, and it will become easier each and every time.

    I want you to be happy. I want you to rejoice and be glad in Me. Give Me praise, as I am praise worthy. Give Me honor and glory and praise, for I am worthy. Put Me first and foremost in your thoughts and your actions, and your life will reflect Me living in you.

    Do these things as obedience to Me, and I will bless you immensely. Remember, when you align your heart with mine, you will be "blessable," and I will bless you.

God

God, I want you to know...

God Wants You to Know...

My child, the one I created on purpose for a purpose, do you trust me? Do you want what I want? Do you see the future I have planned for you? Are you willing to give up everything I ask you to and accept all I have for you? I do not ask you to do this without the help of the Holy Spirit whom I have given you. Give Him complete control of your life, your thoughts, and your actions. My Spirit within you spells success, peace, and victory.

There is no need to go alone in this path I have laid out for you. There is no need to experience failure, fear, or regret when you depend wholly on Me every day in every way. Just, trust, and obey.

I love you.

God

God, I want you to know...

God Wants You to Know...

Holy, holy, holy, merciful and mighty God in three Persons, the blessed Trinity.

I am your heavenly Father, your heavenly Brother, and your heavenly Adviser.

I love you as a father, as one of my own. I love you as a brother. I am your best Friend. I have your back. I love you as a client, someone I advise, instruct, and keep on the straight and narrow path to success and victory.

We are merciful and mighty. We are, we were, and we are to come. We are three in one. We have many names. We are many things to many people. We are all things holy, merciful, and mighty. We are the blessed Trinity. Worship, love, and obey us, and all you desire will come to pass.

We will always love you!

God the Father
Jesus the Son
God the Holy Spirit

God, I want you to know...

God Wants You to Know...

What do you want Me to do in your life? Where do you want Me to take you? If you could do anything and go anywhere, what would it be and where would it be?

Don't worry about the how, the why, the when, and the where. Leave that up to Me. You concern yourself with being ready, being willing, and being able.

Remember to dream (do your routines every day, and I will meet you there).

I have given you a mission, a vision, goals, and dreams. I have given you a heart, a soul, and a body to use for My glory. Put Me first, others next, and yourself last, and I will give you joy unspeakable, full of glory, and you will live life to the fullest. You will go where I send you, do what I ask, and be all you can be in Me.

Just trust and obey. Selah.

God

God, I want you to know...

God Wants You to Know...

　　Hallelujah! Hallelujah! Hallelujah!
　　Lord God Almighty who was, who is, and who is to come! Glory to God in the highest. Praise my holy name, the name above all names, the Way, the Truth and the Life. No man comes unto the Father except by Me.
　　Hallelujah! Hallelujah! Hallelujah!
　　Be still and know that I am God.
　　Listen and obey. Resist the devil, and he will flee. Never give up. Never go it alone.
　　Always put Me first, others second, and yourself last.
　　Selah.

God

God, I want you to know...

God Wants You to Know...

Be still (silently take in my lasting love), and know that I am God.

As you take my love in, you will be able to give it out, as you give it out it will be returned to you, not by those you give it to but by Me.

Do not worry if people love you. I love you. Do not worry if you can love the unlovely. I love them. I will show them My love through you. By loving Me, you will be loving them.

They say, "Love makes the world go round." I say, "Love (is what) makes the world go on their knees." On their knees is where I will save them, promote them, and commission them.

Their mission will be the same as yours: to establish and extend My kingdom.

Start by being still.

Amen.

God

God, I want you to know...

God Wants You to Know...

    In all things, give praise and thanksgiving! I give you an attitude of gratitude, not of faultfinding, complaining, and discord. I give you grace, love, and a sound mind. What do you give me? All I want is your praise and thanksgiving, your loyalty, and your love. I want you to give Me those things. I also want you to give to others as you give to Me. I accept you as you are; others may not. Others may want you to be different, more like them. Don't listen to them. I want you to be more like Me. Strive to be more like Me, your Savior, your Lord, and your best Friend.

    Do all you do as unto the Lord, and you will be happy.

Love,
Papa God

God, I want you to know...

God Wants You to Know...

"Whenever," "whatever," "wherever," and "however" are words I want as responses to My biddings.

I will send you. Your response: "Send me wherever you want me to go, whenever you want me to go."

I want you to give. Your response: "Whatever and however you want me to give, I will give."

I want you to love. Your response: "I will love whomever you want me to love, whenever, wherever, and however you want me to love them."

"I am willing, Lord. I am able, and I am ready for you to use me for your glory. Amen."

Respond to Me this way, and I will use you for My glory.

Amen and amen!

God

God, I want you to know...

God Wants You to Know...

    I want to bless you. I want to give you the desires of your heart. I want to give you all things good. I want to give you more than you can think or imagine. But before I do, I want you to give Me your heart, your soul, and your mind. Your heart I will fill with My love. Your soul I will fill with purpose and longing to be more like Me. Your mind I will control with My thoughts, and fill with wisdom.

    Remember, all that I give, you must give away. Give My love to everyone you meet. Help others to find purpose for their lives and to long for Me. Wisdom is for all who ask. Teach them how to ask Me for wisdom and all things good.

    Also start small end big like I did. I started as a newborn baby and ended up the Savior of the world. This is not your mission but your mission is just as important to Me.

Love you.
Papa God

God, I want you to know...

God Wants You to Know...

Don't do life alone! I did not design you to walk the lonely path. I designed you to walk the path I have already walked, the one that I have strategically placed other believers on to help and support you on your way to Me. I never intended you to do life alone. I never intended you to rely on Me alone. Rely on the people I place on your path for godly wisdom, encouragement, and the love I will give them to give to you. Remember, I have placed you on the paths of others for the same reasons.

Love,
God

God, I want you to know...

God Wants You to Know...

Where I am? Where am I in your life?

Am I first, second, or last? Where am I on your journey? In the beginning, the middle, or the end? Where am I in your future? Can you see Me in your future? I am in you. Everywhere you are, there I am also. I am in all of your life. The best thing for you is to put Me first and others second and yourself last. I am in you, so I am on the whole journey with you, at the beginning to get you started, in the middle helping and encouraging you, and at the end ready to welcome you home.

I am your future. With Me all things are possible. Without Me, there is no hope and no eternal life with Me. Your future is bright, your future is secure, and your future is me!

I love you. I am waiting for you in glory.

Father God

God, I want you to know...

God Wants You to Know...

"Who do you say I am?" you ask. I say you are mine. I say you are the daughter of King Jesus. I say you are able to do all things. You are the head and not the tail. You are first and not last. You are precious to Me. You are My greatest possession. You are the one I love. Come dance with Me. Let Me lead; you follow.

You are My greatest creation, a work of art, My greatest workmanship. You are the reason I sent Jesus to die on the cross.

Today you are ready to be all you can be for Me.

Today is the day you fully commit to becoming available to Me.

Today you and I start the journey I have laid out for you.

Today is the day I have made. Rejoice and be glad in it.

God

God, I want you to know...

God Wants You to Know...

    Bloom where I have planted you. Bring joy to those I have surrounded you with. Be happy and content where you are, but always be ready to move. Where you are is not where you will end up; it is only a rest stop on your journey to life everlasting with Me in glory. Enjoy every day and every opportunity I give you on your journey. The best is yet to come. Get ready, get ready, get ready!

    I will never leave you nor forsake you. Never leave Me nor forsake Me. That would be the easy road; don't take it. Take the hard road, the one that leads to great joy and contentment.

    I love you just the way you are, but that doesn't mean I want you to stay there. Come with Me, My beloved, and you will be blessable, and I will bless you.

    The best is yet to come.

    Hallelujah! Amen.

God

God, I want you to know...

God Wants You to Know...

Fabulous Admirable Victorious OverReaching Love FAVOR.

You have found favor in the eyes of the Lord! You are worthy. You are fabulous, admirable, victorious, and have My overreaching love, which enables you to "reach over" obstacles in your way, to reach over the negativity, to reach over circumstances, and to pull that one out of the miry clay.

Favor can also be unexpected blessings along the way. I love to pour out my favor in the form of blessings on My children. You may not deserve it. You may not even need it. You only need to accept it. Remember, I gave you these things because I love you!

Papa God

God, I want you to know...

God Wants You to Know...

Don't worry about it! You've got this! I've got you, and I am all you need. Just do your best, and trust Me to do the rest. Honor and glorify your Father above, and He will pour out blessings, favor, and wisdom down on you every day of your life.

Do it now. Stop waiting for the perfect time. Start preparing yourself for success. Success comes when you are prepared and you rely on Me. I never said you would have to do it on your own, in your own strength, wisdom, and power. Rely on Me, and together we will establish and extend God's kingdom. With Me your potential is unlimited. There is nowhere we can't go and nothing we cannot accomplish.

Are you in? I am!

Holy Spirit

God, I want you to know...

God Wants You to Know...

    Change your mind, change your attitude, change your ways, and change your life. If you don't change these things, you will stay complacent, self-indulgent, disobedient, and you will settle for less.

    The right changes at the right time will empower you to overcome all the negativity in your life.

    Change your mind when you make decisions that are selfish, self-centered, or self-indulgent. Change your mind, and decide not to do that. Change your attitude; doing good things with the wrong attitude is not pleasing to Me. Change your attitude. Change your ways to be My ways, and you will succeed in all you do for Me. Change your life. Your life will change for the better when you do these things.

    You are on the right path. Keep going, don't quit, and don't slow down.

    I love you.

God

God, I want you to know...

God Wants You to Know...

Do you trust me? Do you believe I am all things to all people? Do you believe I want the best for My children and will do everything in My power to make it so? Do you believe that all things work together for good for those who love Me, honor Me, and obey Me?

Be Transformed and Ready to be Used Spiritually Today **(TRUST)**! Only Begin Every day Yearning to obey **(OBEY)**.

Trust and obey. It is the only way to be happy in Jesus.

Do Your Routines Every day, And I will Meet you there **(DREAM)**.

Very Important, Simple Images of Necessary Steps **(VISIONS)** are what I have given you.

I believe in you. You will reach your God-Ordained Activities of Love **(GOALS)**, which I have given you.

Don't stop, don't give up, start small, and end big!

Abba Father
God

God, I want you to know...

God Wants You to Know...

My child, My child, My child, how do I love thee? Let Me count the ways.

1. I love you by giving you life. Love Me by giving it back to Me.
2. I love you when you are unlovely. Love Me by striving to be better.
3. I love you by giving you freedom. Love Me by living righteously in that freedom.
4. I love you by giving you choices. Love Me by making the right ones.
5. I love you by always being here for you. Love Me by depending on Me and not yourself.
6. I love you just the way you are. You love Me when you are no longer satisfied with that and you strive to become the best you can be for Me.
7. I love you in the dark of night and the light of day. Love Me by trusting Me at all times.
8. I love you now and forever! Love Me back now and forever.

I love you!

God

God, I want you to know...

God Wants You to Know...

LISTEN (Love Is Some Thing Everyone Needs).
Listen and you will hear their cries.
Listen and you will hear the emptiness in their souls.
Listen and you will hear their despair.
LISTEN (Love Is Some Thing Everyone Needs)! They need My love. I need you to give them My love. I need you to show them how much I love them and how much I want them for My own.

Listen and I will instruct you and tell you what to do, when to do it, what to say, when and how to say it, and where I want you to go.

Listen and obey is what I am asking of you today.

TRUST (Transformed, Ready to be Used Spiritually Today) is what I need from you.

God

God, I want you to know...

God Wants You to Know...

You are My beloved. You are My joy. In you I have placed a longing, a longing to be needed, appreciated, and loved. Do not fear; do not be anxious or afraid. I am with you to sustain you, to love you, and be to you everything you need!

The longings I have given you are for a purpose. They are there to propel you into your future of success and not failure, a bright future and not one of darkness and despair.

I am all you need.

DREAM (Do your Routine Every day, And I will meet you there). Never stop dreaming. Your dreams are My dreams, your visions are My visions, and your goals are My goals. That is the way it should be.

Never slow down! Never give up!

Start small; end big.

I've got your back. Keep going.

God

God, I want you to know...

God Wants You to Know...

What do I look like to you? What do I sound like? What do I feel like?

I want you to see Me as your loving Father, one who cares for you, provides for you, reprimands you when needed, and is only a prayer away.

I want you to hear Me every time you listen to Me. I want you to hear the reason I say what I say. I want you to hear the love I put into the words I speak to you. I want you to hear Me in the day-to-day sounds all around you, especially the ones coming from the hearts of the people I have surrounded you with.

I want you to feel Me holding you in My arms. I want you to hear My heart beating. I want you to feel loved by Me. I want you to feel needed, appreciated, and accepted by Me.

I want you to know that I love you.

Abba Father

God, I want you to know...

God Wants You to Know...

"Let my soul sing praises unto you, my Father." Let this be your prayer. Your soul does not use words or music or a melody to sing unto Me. Your soul is your very being and your core belief. It is where I live and breathe and where I am. I didn't create you with a beautiful voice, but I did give you a beautiful soul. I didn't give you the gift of music, but your praises are more coveted by Me than those. Your praises are like beautiful music to My ears. Praise Me by how you live. Praise Me by the way you act. Praise Me by trusting in Me. Praise Me by obeying Me. Praise Me by listening to every word that comes out of my mouth. Praise Me by making a difference in other people's lives. Praise Me by making right choices and living a life of integrity.

Praise God from whom all blessings flow! Amen.

God

God, I want you to know...

God Wants You to Know...

Be careful! Be careful little eyes what you see. Look not at the evil, but look for the good. I am good; look for Me. Seek and you will find Me.

Be careful little ears what you hear. Listen to those I have ordained. I have sent them to encourage, enlighten, and train you up in the way you should go.

Be careful little mouth what you speak. Speak with authority the words I give you. Speak words of life to those whose spirit is dead or wounded. Speak words of encouragement to those whose hope is wavering or gone. Speak words of love to all people I have put in your life.

Be careful little feet where you go. I have a path for you to follow. If there is a fork on the path, you are on the wrong path. Go back, and find the path I am waiting for you on.

In all things, give Me the glory and the praise, and I will guide and direct and bless you all the days of your life.

I love you.

Abba Father

God, I want you to know...

God Wants You to Know...

Wonderful words of life. Words full of wonder and life. These are My words written for you in My Word, the Bible. In the beginning was the Word, and the Word was with God, and the Word was God. I am the Word.

LISTEN (Love Is Something Everyone Needs) to Me, the Word. LIVE (Love Is Vital for Everyone) by My words and LOVE (Love is Our Vision for Everyone) My Word.

Love is where My heart is. Love is where your heart is. To listen, to live and to love are my plans for you.

Listen to My Word, live how it tells you to, and love Me with all your heart.

Read My Word every day, and you will be on your way to accomplishing your dreams, seeing your visions come true, and reaching your goals.

Remember, you do not need to do this alone. I am with you every step of the way.

Love,
The Word
God

God, I want you to know...

God Wants You to Know...

"I surrender all to Jesus. I surrender, I surrender all."

Surrender: to give up; to no longer hold dear; to relinquish control. What do I ask you to surrender? All? What is all? I have given you all things that you have, and now I want them back? Yes! I want back your life, all of it. I want back your joy, all of it. I want back your family, your friends, and your acquaintances. All of them. I want you to relinquish all control of all things in your life. I want you to surrender it all. It is time. Do it now.

Only by surrendering will you truly have all things that I want for you. I have so much more to give you, truly above and beyond all you can think or imagine.

All is a little overwhelming. Start with your heart, and we will go from there.

There is nothing more important for you to do than this.

Love,
Jesus

God, I want you to know...

God Wants You to Know...

This is the day the Lord has made. Let us rejoice and be glad in it! Yesterday is gone, tomorrow is not promised, so live today fully unto Me.

Regrets are Satan's way of keeping us stuck in the past. Forgive, forget, and move on. I forgave you before you even did anything wrong. Your sins were forgiven—past, present, and future. Live in that truth. Live in that freedom. Live in that hope. Live like Love is Our Vision for Everyone (LOVE). Living isn't about loving oneself. It is about loving others. Don't get stuck in the past fretting, regretting, and dwelling in unforgiveness. Live every day in My glorious hope, grace, and mercy, My everlasting love.

Resist the devil, and he will flee. Remember, all I have for you is more than Satan ever has to offer. Don't fall for his tricks, and never, never, never believe his lies!

Love,
God your Father from whom all blessings flow

God, I want you to know...

God Wants You to Know...

Know no other way. There is no other way to heaven except by Me. I am the way, the only way.
I am the way to happiness, the only way.
I am the way to success, the only way.
I am the way to truth, the only way.
I am the way to life everlasting, the only way.
There are other ways that seem like they will get you to happiness, success, the truth, and even to heaven; but those ways are not My ways and will end in sadness, failure, lies from the pit, and hell. Don't be tricked into believing that you can accomplish anything on your own. You cannot; you need Me. You need to follow Me. I will make your crooked paths straight. I will remove all obstacles, making your paths smooth. Follow Me, for there is no other way.

The Way, the Truth and the Life,
God your Father

God, I want you to know...

God Wants You to Know...

Put Me first, second, and last. Put Me above all others. Put Me before all things. Put Me first, second, and last, and I will put you where you need to be when you need to be there. I will give you many opportunities to honor and glorify Me in all that you do and all that you say. Look for those opportunities. Look for those ways. I will show you those everlasting ways in which I will lead you.

Be not afraid, be not anxious, but be bold, be assured of My presence, be courageous, be assured of My power in you, and be victorious. Be assured of My victory I have already won.

Look up! Look at me! Look to the future.

Make Me your everything, and I will make you like Me.

My daughter, you can do this. You need to do this. Trust and obey, for there is no other way to be happy in Jesus than to trust and obey. I love you.

Abba Father

God, I want you to know...

God Wants You to Know...

Just as I am without one plea, what does that mean to Me? It means that you come to Me with an open heart. You are open to whatever I desire to give you and to do My bidding without hesitation. This is what I want; this is what I desire from you. Stop trying to control your life. Stop trying to do life on your own. Come to Me just as you are. You are enough. You are willing; I can work with that. You are able; I can work with that. You are ready; I can work with that. Let me do My work in you so you can do My work here on earth.

Don't be discouraged, distraught, or disobedient, but be encouraged, joyful, and obedient.

I accept you just as you are, but I don't want you to stay that way. Let Me change you into the child you were always meant to be.

I love you and am very proud to call you My child.

Father God

God, I want you to know...

God Wants You to Know...

    I want to tell you that I love you and am very proud of you. I want to thank you for helping others without question or hesitation. I know that I can trust you, so I will be asking more of you. Get ready, get ready, get ready!

    One way to get ready is by asking Me for more of Me in your heart and in your life. Another way is to DREAM (Do Your Routine Every day, And I will Meet you there). Embracing the dreams I give you shows Me that you want what I want; that is good.

    Don't run on ahead of Me. Don't lag behind; just walk beside Me all the way every day, hand in hand, with the same goals, dreams, and purpose. My plan is perfect for you. Embrace all that will get you to where you need to be. There will be waiting, disappointment, and maybe even discouragement along the way, but keep going, keep trusting, and have faith. We will get there—together.

God

God, I want you to know...

God Wants You to Know...

Stop. Stop running to others for only what I can give you. Run to Me; run into My arms I am holding out for you. Run into My embrace, and enjoy being with Me and Me only; I am all you need. Turn your mind off, turn off your need to know and understand, and trust Me. Enjoy the moment that turns into a lifestyle that turns into eternity. I cherish the time we spend together each day. I cherish the thought that we are better together, that we need each other, and we will not do life alone.

You cannot get what I can give you anywhere else other than in the time you spend with Me, being STILL (Silently Taking In my Lasting Love) and being wholly Mine. **KNOW** (Know No Other Way) My love for you, My never-ending, everlasting, always abounding love for you.

I am your God. I am all you need. Stop running to other sources, and run to me...

I will love you forever and will never fail you.

Papa God

God, I want you to know...

God Wants You to Know...

Get ready, get ready, get ready!

I am doing a great work in you, and the time is coming for you to flourish. No more complacency, no more time to settle, no more thinking only of yourself, no more laziness, and no more disobedience! No more. From now on, I declare over you a spirit of love and compassion over others, an urgency to be about your father's business, a desire for above and beyond, a work ethic that will make Me proud, and the desire to **OBEY** (Only Begin Every day Yearning) Me. This is My declaration.

"How do I get ready?" you ask. Keep doing what you are doing, and I will show you what to do next. Try not to get ahead of Me. You are called to follow after Me. Let Me lead you in the way everlasting. Be willing, ready, and available, and I will use you for My glory.

I am so excited for you.

Love,
God

God, I want you to know...

God Wants You to Know...

No fear! Do not be afraid. **FEAR** is False Evidence Against Righteousness. I don't give you a spirit of fear, and I never will. I give you a spirit of righteousness and a sound mind. Satan, your adversary, offers you a spirit of fear and condemnation. Don't accept it. Don't even open that door, not even a crack. All Satan has to do is to get you to open the door to his lies, just enough for him to shove in doubt. If he can get you to doubt My word, doubt My love, or even doubt My existence, he is in. Close the door and lock it. Lock it with truth, the wonderful words of truth. Satan cannot stand the truth; he will flee.

Replace fear with truth, love, and obedience. God's Word, My love, the Holy Spirit's bidding is all you need to resist the devil and have a victorious life in Me.

Your heavenly Father,
God almighty and full of glory

God, I want you to know...

God Wants You to Know...

    Don't take anything for granted. You are not promised sun without rain, life without pain, and success without struggles. I call you to take the straight and narrow path, the only path that leads to Me, to victory and happiness.

    Don't assume that this path is free of heartaches, challenges, and situations that you will not welcome. But be assured that everything you encounter on this path is there for a reason. It is there to strengthen you, to grow your faith and to teach you how to make the right choices. Do not be afraid of things to come. I am with you till the end and then forever as there is no "end."

    Depend on Me for everything, trust Me in everything, and love Me until the day you die—the day you come to live with Me in glory forever and ever. Amen.

    Until then, just trust and obey.

    I love you.

God

God, I want you to know...

God Wants You to Know...

"Light my way," you pray. "Light up my heart with your love, light up my mind with your wisdom, and light up my life with your presence. Be the light that disperses my darkness. Be the light that warms my heart, igniting compassion and love for all!"

Yes! My answer is yes! I will light up the way I want you to walk in. All other ways lead to darkness. I will light up your heart with My love and compassion. Wisdom is yours for the asking, but My presence is yours always. I will never leave you nor forsake you. Yes, I am the Light that warms your heart, igniting love and compassion for all.

Now I want to ask you to do something for Me. I want you to trust Me with all your heart and to not lean on your own understanding. Will you do that? Also, obey Me even when it is hard and you don't want to. Will you do that? There is no other way to be happy in Jesus than to trust and obey Me.

God

God, I want you to know...

God Wants You to Know...

VISION: Very Important Spiritual Images Of Necessary steps.

I have given you visions, dreams, and goals. Work on the visions I have given you first.

1. Having an attitude of gratitude at all times! This is so important! Ungrateful people will go nowhere. Grateful people succeed in all they do for the honor and glory of My name.
2. Moving My truth from your head to your heart to your hands. You feel you are stuck at your heart, but you are not. You are just not ready yet to move on to your hands. Be patient. All things always work for good for those who love Me.
3. To be generous and compassionate like Jesus. Make this one a priority, and I will show you the ways in which I want you to do this.
4. To listen to and love people of all ages to give them a better quality of life. This is not only My vision, but it is My dream for you and will be the reason you achieve your goals. Never give up and never give in.

Love,
God

God, I want you to know...

God Wants You to Know...

"Glory, glory, glory to the Father and to the Son. Holy is your name, O Lord. Holy are you. Holy, holy, holy, Lord God Almighty. Hallelujah! Hallelujah! Hallelujah!"

There is power in your praises. There is power in My name, and there is power in the blood of the lamb that was slain.

This is the power you have access to 24-7. There is no limit to My power. The limitation is only in you. You need faith to receive My power. When you don't have enough faith, you need to grow your faith. You grow your faith by using it. The more you use it, the more you will have. The more faith you have, the more power you will have. This power can be used against Satan and the battle he is waging against you and Me. With this power, you will have victory each and every time.

Keep your praises coming. It shows that you love Me.

I love you,
God

God, I want you to know...

God Wants You to Know...

A praise to God:

    As smoke rises to heaven, may my praises rise also. As my praises rise to heaven, may my heart rise also. As my heart rises to heaven, may my soul also rise.

    As rain comes down from heaven, may your blessings rain down. As your blessings rain down on us, may we bless others. As we bless others, may they bless you, and may all we do honor you.

    As the earth grows and produces, may your children grow and produce also. As your children grow and produce, so may your truth. As your truth grows and produces, so may your kingdom do so also.

    Lord Jesus, I praise your holy name. I give you my heart and my soul to do with as it pleases you. I accept the blessings you bestow, and I will live by your truth. I will accept your mission for my life: to establish and extend God's kingdom here on earth.

Love,
(Your name)

God, I want you to know...

God Wants You to Know...

    Faith is something we all need. Without it, we are nothing. There are many things we put our faith in every day. We go to bed at night having faith that we will wake up in the morning. We eat having faith that the food will sustain us and keep us alive. We go to work having faith that we will get paid for what we do and that it will sustain us until the next paycheck. We put our faith in things and people without even thinking, but I want you to put your faith in Me first and foremost. When you put your faith in Me, it will do the most good. I will reward your faithfulness with love, grace, mercy, and peace. Trust in Me for your every need. Put your faith in Me, and do not waver, and your joy will be full. Remember, only I can see the future and know all truth, and only I am worthy of your faith and trust. I will never let you down.

Love,
God

God, I want you to know...

God Wants You to Know...

    Talk to Me when you don't know what to do. Talk to Me when you don't feel adequate. Talk to Me when you are blue and don't know what to do. I am here. I am listening. I hear what you say. I understand what you mean. I get you. Do not be afraid to confide in Me. Your thoughts, your concerns, even your fears are safe with Me. Talk to Me as your Brother. Confide in Me as your Confidant (the Holy Spirit that I am), and make your requests known to Me, your loving Father.
    There is not a day that passes that I don't yearn for a conversation with you, a walk in the garden where I can tell you, you are mine and I am yours, and our joy can be complete.
    Talk to Me. Walk with Me every day in every way so that your joy will be complete.
    Come to the garden alone, soon and often. I am waiting there for you.

God the Father, God the Son, and God the Spirit

God, I want you to know...

God Wants You to Know...

Write these words: "I am all you need. I need to be all you want. Whenever you need something, come to Me. Whenever I want something, I will come to you. To be willing, able, and available is all I ask. Sometimes My children need the love that only you can give them from Me. Sometimes My people need an understanding that only you can impart to them from Me. Sometimes My chosen ones need an example of how to be that can only come from Me to them through you."

Do you ever wonder why you are where you are, doing what you are doing, and living the way you are living? Do you ever wonder why I don't tell you? Faith and trust. I need your faith, and I need to know that you trust Me. It is enough that I know all things. It is enough that you live by faith and trust Me for the answers to these questions to be yours when you need them. Until then, just trust and obey.

I love you,
God

God, I want you to know...

God Wants You to Know...

    A shield of faith, I give you for your protection from the enemy. As long as you keep your faith in Me, you are protected from the fiery darts of the enemy. What do I mean by this?

    When Satan throws his fiery darts of contentment, doubt, fear, and complacency at you, you will put up your shield of faith and stand firm. You will not give in to self-indulgence and disobedience. You will tell him to flee, and he will. It is not that Satan sees the shield or you standing firm behind it, but he sees Me standing behind you, and he has no power over Me.

    Whenever you are tempted with contentment, doubt, fear, or anything else, put your faith in Me, for I am standing right behind you.

    I know it can be scary and Satan can be intimidating, but each time you do it, your faith will grow, and it will become easier and easier!

I love you,
God

God, I want you to know...

God Wants You to Know...

To know Me is to love Me. The more you know Me, the greater your love for Me will be. You have known about Me all your life, starting with Sunday school, then church, then Bible camp, and so on. I want you to get to know Me intimately, to know Me as I know you. I know everything there is to know about you: your life, your heart, your longings, your desires, your hopes and dreams—everything, even things you don't know yet. I want you to get to know Me as the lover of your soul, the one who treasures you above all others, the one that thinks of you day and night, and the one that yearns for your love and devotion.

There seems to be a mountain of fear and trepidation between you and Me. Put your faith in me, and that mountain will fall into the sea. Put your faith in Me, and together we will be the best team we can be.

Getting to know Me is a goal I give you today. Reach out to Me to obtain this goal.

Love,
God

God, I want you to know...

God Wants You to Know...

Warmth comes from fire like when I put a fire in your belly, you feel the warmth of My love. Warmth comes from an embrace. When you run into My arms into My embrace, you feel the warmth of My love for you. Warmth can also come from you feeling good about yourself—the feeling you get when you are doing My will and living wholeheartedly for Me.

The next step is to take this warmth and give it to the cold and lonely, rejected and scorned. Who? You say you don't know anyone like that. Look around; those people are everywhere. Everyone I love, but don't know Me yet, are shivering for the warmth of My love.

Everyone I am not walking with on the path of life is lonely. The rejected and scorned are oftentimes those believers who no longer fit in with their family and friends, the ones that are no longer understood. Move closer to them so they can feel My warmth. I love them.

God

God, I want you to know...

God Wants You to Know...

Deep breath. Breathe in my love; breathe out my love. Breathe in My mercy; breathe out My mercy. Breathe in My grace; breathe out My grace. With every breath you take, remember who gave you that breath—the breath of life. Remember Me and the love, mercy, and grace that I impart to you every day.

Everyone you meet every day is looking for what you have—my love, My mercy, and My amazing grace.

Look for ways to pass these gifts I have given you to those you come in contact with each day. Love them by being attentive to them. Show them mercy by accepting them for who they are, and give them grace because I ask you to. Remember, "But for My grace, there go you."

Gifts are meant to be given. The more you give, the more that will be given back to you. Love, mercy, and grace give I to thee. Give freely.

Love,
God

God, I want you to know...

God Wants You to Know...

Smell the sweet aroma of My love. See the product of the work of My hands. Feel the joy unspeakable and full of glory that floods your soul. Experience all I have for you here on earth and later in heaven with Me. Life and death are in the tongue, speak life. Speak life when you feel like dying. Speak life when you are discouraged and downtrodden. Speak life when you feel lonely and worthless. Speak wonderful, beautiful words of life.

Don't let your feelings dictate your life. Just because you "feel" a certain way, that doesn't mean that that is the way life really is; it just means that you are trying to control things. Give complete control of your life to the Holy Spirit, and He will show you the truth, the way, and the life you are intended to live.

Put your trust in Me (The Three in One), and you will have joy unspeakable and full of glory, and your life will be worth living. I love you.

God

God, I want you to know...

God Wants You to Know...

    Resist Every Sinful Tension **(REST)** by resting in Me. Come to Me, ye who are burdened and heavy-laden. Give Me your burdens and those things that are weighing you down. Uncertainty, unclarity, doubt, fear, whatever you are dealing with right now, give them all to Me. I died to cleanse you from all unrighteousness and give you a new heart—a heart full of love, faith, and a longing for righteousness like nothing you have ever experienced before.

    With this new heart, you are able to love others more than you do yourself. Have faith in Me, and trust Me to do all I have ever promised that I will do.

    You are equipped with the Holy Spirit to help you with your everyday living experience. Give complete control to Him, and you will soar and have enough energy to do all I have for you to do each day. I love you.

Papa God

God, I want you to know...

God Wants You to Know...

    Sweetness, loveliness, and righteousness are the attributes I long for you to have. I want to replace all the tartness, ugliness, and unrighteousness that you were born into with these attributes.

    Sweet, sweet child of mine, I adore you. You are as lovely as the morning dew and as refreshing as the evening rain. You are in right standing with Me, forgiven and washed as white as snow. I call you righteous!

    Your mission is to establish and extend My kingdom. Do that by being the sweet where there is tartness, being lovely in spite of all the ugliness, and being righteous in a very not righteous world.

    If when they see you, they see Me, that will make all the difference in the world.

    Keep praying that My kingdom come and My will be done on earth as it is in heaven, and it will be.

Love,
God

God, I want you to know...

God Wants You to Know...

Peace like a river flowing through your mind; joy like an ocean crashing against the walls of your heart; love enveloping you like a warm fuzzy blanket.

These are things I give you, things that I lavish on you because you are My child and I love you. I know you have questions that need answering, concerns that need addressing, and wants that need to be fulfilled—all in due time.

Do not fret or worry about the things you have no control over. Give those things to Me. Do not be anxious for tomorrow. I will take care of your future. Do not doubt My desire for you to have the best life I can give you.

The best gift I have for you is faith. Faith is what you use instead of worry, anxiousness, and doubt. Faith comes by hearing the Word of God. I only ask you to listen, trust, and obey, for there is no other way to be happy in Jesus than to trust and obey. I give you My word.

Love,
God

God, I want you to know...

God Wants You to Know...

  Reflection: that which is seen in a glass or a mirror, an image of a person looking at a glass or mirror. When you look at Me, I reflect the image I see, and it looks a lot like Me. When I see you looking to Me for everything, I see Me fulfilling all your needs and supplying your wants too. When you want what I want, you will get what you want. Reflection can also be looking back on what has already happened and reminiscing about all the great things we have done together. I have used you in the past and will do so in the future. Reflecting is a great tool to use for My glory, but be careful not to be stuck in the past. Your future is bright and waiting for you.

  Do you trust me? Do you really, really trust me? Now is not the time to reflect but to act. Now is the time to trust and obey. No matter what happens, I am here for you. I've got your back.

God

God, I want you to know...

God Wants You to Know...

Support: the thing that holds up another thing or in this case, a person that holds up another person in prayer and in love. I support you so that you are able to support others. The need for support is always there and always will be.

How do I want you to support My children in need of your support right now? Start by being available day and night; nothing you have to do is as important as this. Use encouraging words. Take the time to speak into their lives: hope, joy, peace, and love. Be creative; do things for them that you would like someone to do for you if you were in the same situation. Be a blessing to their children. Any distraction from their current situation would be a blessing. Communicate daily, one way or another. Make sure they know you are thinking of them and that you care deeply.

I ask you to do these things because these are the things I am going to do as their heavenly Parent. Let's do this together.

Father God

God, I want you to know...

God Wants You to Know...

    I am interested in you. I am interested in your thoughts and actions, the reasons why you do what you do. I am interested in your story and what makes you, you. I am interested in your life and how you live it. I want you to be interested in the people and their lives that are all around you.

    Be interested in their story: how they are now and how they used to be.

    Find out all you can about them: what makes them tick, what makes them happy, what makes them sad, and what makes them glad. Be interested in their day-to-day. Get involved in their lives, and it will make your life very interesting. When you invest in others, I will invest in you. When I invest in you, you will become rich—rich in wisdom, rich in confidence, and rich in relationships. I will pour out My Fabulous, Admirable, Victorious, OverReaching (FAVOR) love on you.

Love,
God

God, I want you to know...

God Wants You to Know...

    Composition: an article composed of thoughts and ideas, relating to a subject that matters. I wrote such an article that is called "The Word of God." It is a book about Me, My Son, and our earthly children. It is a subject that matters most of all. The story I like most of all is the one they called the Easter Story—the one where My son takes on the sins of the world and where He is crucified, He dies, and is risen. He is now sitting here at My right hand.

    There is now no condemnation. You are set free by the blood of the Lamb, My Son, Jesus. Freedom is being able to compose your own story, your thoughts, and your ideas about a subject that matters: you! Write it down as you live it. Write it down as I give you the words to say. Your testimony is an article that will make a difference in many lives just as My story did. Go for it.

Love,
God

God, I want you to know...

God Wants You to Know...

Fire, burning light, heat, warmth, desire, necessity, useful, welcoming, lovely, comforting, and wanted—these are the words I use to describe what I want to see you become and to have.

Fire, My fire burning in your soul, creating heat (fuel) energy to do My will. Light, what I am, shining on you so you will not stumble. Warmth, the feeling people get when they are around you.

Desire, mine and yours, to be all we can be for and with each other. Necessity, without Me you are nothing, and the need will not be met. I need you. Useful—being used by Me. Welcoming every opportunity to serve Me is a trait I love about you. The Holy Spirit living in you makes you lovely and comforting and allows you to be and to do these for others. Wanted: never doubt how much you are wanted. I want every good thing for you, especially each and every one of these things, and more. This is only the beginning. Get ready, get ready, get ready!

Sincerely,
God

God, I want you to know...

God Wants You to Know...

Circle: a group of people with shared interests or acquaintances. As a circle of friends, I have a special circle I want you to belong in. The members of this circle need you as much as you need them. I will be in the center of this circle, burning like a candle, giving off light and warmth. As long as you stay in the circle, you will be in My will, and all will be well. You will be able to leave the circle when I don't need you to be there any longer. Then I will give you a new circle to be in. When you go to a new circle, make sure I am in the center giving off light and heat. Jesus's love will be present, and all will be well. Sometimes you will be in a circle within a circle. That's okay, as long as you can feel My presence. The circles represent your dreams, visions, and goals. They will overlap or envelope each other, and that's the way it should be. As long as I am present and you are in My will, all will be well with your soul.

Sincerely,
God

God, I want you to know...

God Wants You to Know...

    I am the Truth, the Way, and the Light. No man comes to the Father except by Me; there is no other way. Many people believe they can do it on their own. Other people believe their religious beliefs will get them to Me. Other people believe there is no need to get to Me or heaven, where I am. Either way, the truth is there is only one way, and I am that way. Now how do we get the truth to those that need it, the ones that believe the lies and those who make up the lies? One way is to Love them into the kingdom, unconditional love is the key that opens that door. Another way is to be My hands and feet here on earth. Helping them to experience My love where they are at is another key. One of the most important ways is to be a testimony to My grace and mercy. Some people just need to be told I am the only way. I give you many keys, go now and open the doors to My kingdom for the ones we love.

Sincerely,
God

God, I want you to know...

God Wants You to Know...

Tears, I know tears. I shed many, many tears in the garden that night. Wet, salty, and sometimes bloodstained, they were for you and all mankind. The tears that washed away the sins of the world by what I would do the next day. The tears of anguish, knowing that for many I was going to die in vain. Tears of excitement for those who would accept Me as their Savior and become My children. Tears of dread knowing what was going to happen, and tears of joy for the victory that was won. Tears I give to you to shed for your fellow man. Tears because you know what will happen to them without Me.

Tears of expectation that they will accept Me, and tears of joy when they do.

My love is as wide as the ocean and as deep as the sea. There is nowhere they can go that I cannot see. My love will find them and bring them to Me through your tears. Amen!

Love,
God

God, I want you to know...

God Wants You to Know...

Blemish: a stain or mark on something; an unwanted sin in a clean heart or mind; something that is not easily removed. Adam and Eve were blemished when they ate the apple. Lucifer was blemished when he fell from heaven! The whole creation was blemished by these acts of sin against Me. It breaks My heart to see My children struggling to remove or clean the blemishes they were born with. If they would only come to Me, I would wash them white as snow. I will replace their blemishes with my love, My presence, and My Holy Spirit. It breaks My heart to see My children struggle with trying to remove or clean the blemishes they have acquired since they have become My children. Stop struggling. You have been forgiven. Your sins have been washed away; you are white as snow. All blemishes are gone forever. Satan wants you to believe you have to repent over and over. No!

My grace and My mercy are sufficient for you. No more struggling, no more doubting! Only trusting and believing and taking Me at My word.

Your heavenly Father,
God

God, I want you to know...

God Wants You to Know...

Smell, the sense of smell.

Smell the aroma of My love, the aroma of My peace and joy and longing for companionship with you. It is a beautiful thing; it's like the fresh, clean air after a rain, the smell of burning wood of a campfire, or freshly baked bread. Use your senses to detect Me in your everyday life. I remember the smell of the expensive perfume Mary anointed My head with. I will never forget that act of worship and adornment. I long to smell the flowers in the garden where you used to come so often to walk and be with Me.

The smell of your sweet presence still lingers there.

I also remember the smell of Lazarus as he stepped out of the grave, the smell of death and decay, the smell that gave way to victory and life. Use your sense of smell to detect Me in your everyday life, and enjoy My sweet, sweet presence.

I love you.

God

God, I want you to know...

God Wants You to Know...

And this too will pass. Hang in there, and keep going. Don't slow down. Don't give up. Choose faith over fear, love over hatred, peace over confusion, and victory over defeat. Choose Me over friends, family, and religion. Fear, hatred, confusion, and defeat are Satan's rewards for you when you listen to him and believe his lies and when you obey him instead of Me.

Faith, love, peace, and victory are rewards I give you when you listen to Me and believe My truth and obey Me.

Your friends, family, and all the religion in the world cannot give you what I can give you. When you choose Me, you get eternal life, joy; unspeakable and full of glory, peace that flows like a river in your soul, and companionship incomparable to anything you have ever experienced.

When you need a friend, choose Me. When you need someone to fight your battles, choose Me. When you need someone to lean on, choose Me.

I am here for you, always!

Love,
Papa God

God, I want you to know...

God Wants You to Know...

Time is on your side. Time is for you and not against you. Spend it wisely; don't waste it.

Everyone has the same amount of time, twenty-four hours each and every day. Make every minute count. There is a time for everything. Time is of the essence. The most important way to spend your time is with Me. Cherish every minute you spend with Me. Equally important is the time you spend with others, sharing My love, touching their souls, and just listening to them. Remember, Love Is SomeThing Everyone Needs **(LISTEN)**. Spend time on yourself! This is very important.

Spending time doing what you want to do, what makes you feel good, what enriches your soul is not being selfish; it is being wise. Take time every day to be with Me first and foremost, then spend time with or for yourself and those I have put in your life. Time is eternal but also fleeting. You can't get it back once you have spent it. So spend your time wisely, be prudent, and live in a timely manner.

Love,
God

God, I want you to know...

God Wants You to Know...

The wind obeys My commands. So should you. The wind listens to My voice. So should you. The wind responds to My desires. So should you.

Obedience is the one thing you can choose to do that results in My blessing you, your life, and everyone around you.

Listening to my voice will result in you knowing what I am like, who I am, and why I love you.

For you to respond to My desires brings Me much joy. Like when we are dancing and you let Me lead, when I turn this way and you follow, and I turn that way and you keep in step. Life is a dance. Listen to the music of the wind, and sway with Me.

The wind can also be very destructive: blowing against the waves, making them crash against the shore, and destroying everything on their path. Hurricanes, tornadoes, and tsunamis are caused by the wind. Heed not the wind that is out of control but the wind that I control.

Sincerely,
God

God, I want you to know...

God Wants You to Know...

Stain: a mark or blemish; something impossible to remove.

Sin stains the heart—sins like rebellion, disobedience, hate, and anything that goes against My principles and My way of living and loving. There is only one way to remove the stain of being human, of being born into a world of sin, and that is to be cleansed by the blood of the Lamb.

My Son, Jesus, came to earth to die so you could be cleansed from all unrighteousness. Ask Him to come into your heart and to cleanse you and heal your broken and contrite heart. There is no stain or sin that He can't get out and make you as white as snow. When I take your sins, I give you peace, joy, love, and sonship. As a child of the Most High God, you have access to everything I own, which is everything in heaven and on earth. All of heaven rejoices when you receive Jesus as your Savior. Do it today, and don't delay. I am waiting to welcome you into My family and give you many gifts.

I long for you.

God

God, I want you to know...

God Wants You to Know...

Overwhelmed: to be defeated completely; to be given too much of something.

Overwhelmed is the feeling you get when you do life on your own, alone, struggling, and drowning.

I never meant for you to live that way. Let Me help you—no, let Me do it for you. Let Me live My life, My dreams, and My goals through you. Want what I want, desire what I desire, and love the way I love. To do this, I will require you to give up all control, all thoughts of how things should be done, and all suggestions on how to do things your way. It will be My way or the highway. All or nothing.

I love you! I am waiting for you to give Me complete control of your life and accept the freedom that comes with it.

You will be free from condemnation, feelings, and emotions you now have no control over and a life that is going nowhere. I will overwhelm you with My love, My purpose, and a wonderful future. Put Me in control of your life, and you will see.

Love,
God

God, I want you to know...

God Wants You to Know...

Burning desire is what I have for you. A desire to see you become more like Me every day in every way. A desire to communicate with you on a personal level where when I talk, you listen; when you talk, I listen; and where we can talk about everything that is in our minds and hearts. I am very interested in you. Yes, I know your every thought. I know what you will do before you do it, but I still want you to tell Me your burning desires! What are you interested in? What do you want to do more than anything else? What are your burning desires? Make them your goals. Set out to reach them one by one. Write them down and reaffirm them every day. Reaching goals is important. They will help you accomplish all I have for you to do. I don't ask you to do this on your own. Let's do it together. Let's make My plans your plans, My dreams your dreams, My burning desire your burning desire. Let's do this!

I Love you.

God

God, I want you to know...

God Wants You to Know...

Sacrifice: the act of giving something of value up for the sake of something else regardless if it's more important or worthy.

I sacrificed My son on the cross for something I regarded as more important: you! You are worthy of My sacrifice, My love, and My devotion. I have dreams and visions for you, plans to give you hope and a future worth living, and I yearn for you to sacrifice your current way of living for a new life in Me, a better life, one worthy of My presence, one worthy of My sacrifice and yours.

You may see your life now as valuable, but the life I died to give is so much more valuable. When you live life with Me, for Me, and make it all about Me, you and I will make a difference in many lives. There are many people all around you that need us and the sacrifices we will make for them—sacrifices of our time, our energy, and ourselves. They are important and worthy of our love.

Love,
God

God, I want you to know...

God Wants You to Know...

Bask: to revel in and make the most of something pleasing, to lie exposed to warmth and light. Bask in Me, in My light, My presence, and the warmth of My love for you. Revel in My glory, My wisdom, and My discernment. Every day, bask in Me first before the trials come, before your day starts, and before you try doing things your way. There is no better way to do life than to do it with Me, and there is no other way to do life with Me than to bask in My presence and to revel in and make the most of pleasing Me. It pleases Me to see you lying in the warmth and light of My presence, taking in My gifts, which I want to give you every day. Gifts of strength and courage, confidence and wisdom, and the ability to make the right choices and be successful and victorious in whatever comes your way. Bask in My glory, put your faith and trust in Me, live life to the fullest, and I will be pleased and very proud to call you My child.

Papa God

God, I want you to know...

God Wants You to Know...

There is also a time in your life that is the turning point, where you turn from listening to others to only listening to Me, where you turn from obeying others to obeying only Me. A time where you turn from depending on yourself to depending on Me only. A time for reconciling your differences, confessing your sins, seeking forgiveness, and living wholly consecrated to Me. A time of rejoicing, rejuvenation, and freedom.

All these things I promise will come. Get ready, get ready, get ready.

The choices you make will determine your destiny. It is up to you to decide what to do and when to do it. It is up to Me to honor your decisions and to be there for you every step of the way.

Don't stop now. Never give up! Keep going. The victory is yours. Go get it.

I love you.

Father God

God, I want you to know...

God Wants You to Know...

Exalted: to be high and lifted up, worthy of praise and adoration.

I will be exalted among the nations. I will be exalted in the earth. I long to be exalted in the hearts of My children, those who believe in Me, and I reside in their hearts now and forevermore. Hallelujah!

To be exalted is to be loved and received.

To be exalted is to be thought of first and foremost, to be set on a pedestal and set apart as holy, and to glorify, to magnify, and to love with one's whole heart. Exalt Me, and I will in return exalt you. I will lift you up and place you on a pedestal, and I will give you my praise and adoration and love. I will place you first and foremost in My plans for you, the ones that give you a hope and a future. To be exalted is not to be equal with Me but to be happy and proud of how you are living. When you exalt Me in everything you do, it makes Me happy and very proud of you.

I love and exalt you.

God

God, I want you to know...

God Wants You to Know...

    I will take care of you! I will take care of you when you are sick. I will take care of you when you are weary. I will take care of you when you feel all alone. Cast all your cares on Me, for I care for you. I have cared for you even before you were born. I had a plan for you, for good and not for evil, a plan for a future—a future with Me.

    Satan also has a plan—a plan full of evil and destruction, a plan for a future with him in darkness. The choice is up to you. Choose Me, and I will give you everlasting life and eternity in heaven. I will take care of you, and you will live life to the fullest, filled with glory and honor and joy unspeakable. Choose not to choose Me, and you close the door on all I yearn to do for you. I cannot make the choice for you. I can only be patient and wait for you with open arms.

    I am the Truth, the Way, and the Life. No man comes to the Father except by Me. Invite Me into your heart, and I will cleanse you from all unrighteousness, and you will be made white as snow. You will become My child, and I will be your heavenly Father, and no one will be able to pluck you out of My hand.

    The choice is yours. I will be waiting for you.

    I will always love you.

God

God, I want you to know...

God Wants You to Know...

Respect: due regard for the feelings, wishes, and rights of others; the feeling of deep admiration for someone elicited by their abilities, qualities, or achievements.

When you respect others, you respect Me. When you respect Me, others will respect you.

Respect can be demanded or earned. I earn your respect by being perfect, holy, and loving, a good, good father. I demand your respect by rewarding you when you obey Me, by fulfilling your requests, and by answering your prayers.

Honor, praise, and adoration are ways we can respect each other and all others. Give someone a place of honor in your heart and life today. Praise someone for their abilities, qualities, and achievements today. Make your adoration known to someone today. Earn someone's respect in how you act, how you love them, and by having a good attitude at all times.

I respect you, admire you, and I love you. Go respect others as you respect yourself.

Your loving heavenly Father,
God

God, I want you to know...

God Wants You to Know...

Interruption—an act, utterance, or a period of time that stops the continuous progress of an activity or process.

Life is a process, and there will be interruptions now and then. Like when I ask you to stop and think about what you are doing or when I ask you to stop and think about where you are going. When you stop and think things through, you will make wise decisions and will welcome the interruption. Sometimes you are doing good works out of obligation, not out of love. Sometimes you are going down the path of life all alone, doing things on your own without Me. I send interruptions to get your attention to get you to come back to Me and start your journey over this time with Me. An interruption can be a period of time where nothing goes right. It may be words spoken on My behalf that stop you in your tracks and show you a better way. Whatever it is, know that I do it for your good and because I love you.

Sincerely,
Father God

God, I want you to know...

God Wants You to Know...

Trust: a firm belief in the reliability, truth, ability, or strength of someone or something.

Do you believe I am reliable, truthful, able to do all things, and strong enough to fight your battles? Do you find My love to be reliable and truthful? Do you believe I have the ability to love you no matter what? Can you feel how strong and sincere My love is for you? When you can answer yes to all these questions, trust will not be an issue for you.

I believe in you! You have shown yourself reliable to obey Me when I have asked you to. Being truthful is very important to you as is finding out the truth. I have given you great abilities, and you get your strength from relying on Me. I trust you. I believe in your love for Me. It is strong and is able to break down the strongholds of the evil one with truth.

Trust and obedience are required for a happy life in Me. Trust Me and obey, and we will both be happy for eternity.

I love you.

God

God, I want you to know...

God Wants You to Know...

Step: to lift and set down one foot after the other in order to walk somewhere or move to a new position.

When you take a step toward Me, do it with a leap of faith. When you take the steps that are necessary to realize your dreams, take them with a leap of faith. When you take steps toward your goals, take them with a leap of faith. Remember, faith comes by continually hearing the Word of God. Listen to Me, hear My words, and obey My voice. Walk with Me step-by-step on your journey called life! Each step is a choice, each choice is a decision, and each decision is a leap of faith. Don't be content with where you are. I have so much more for you! Don't be willing to settle for what you have now. I have so much more for you. Don't be happy just taking care of yourself. I have so much more for you!

Step out (with a leap of faith), and find out. Your future with Me in complete control is far better than you can ever imagine.

Let us walk this journey together. I will lead.

God

God, I want you to know...

God Wants You to Know...

Beginning: the point in time or space at which something starts.

In the beginning, I created all things. In the beginning, all things worshipped Me. In the beginning, there was no sin—only love and perfection. In the beginning, all was good.

A lot has happened since the beginning. Things are not perfect anymore. Because of My adversary, Satan, people get to choose who they worship and who they don't. Sin is rampant, and love is disappearing. The earth and its inhabitants are deteriorating at surprisingly fast rates.

There will be a new earth and a new heaven—a new beginning for all those who believe in Me, accept Me as their Savior, and live a new life here on earth until it passes away or I come back for My own.

Make today the point in time that you start a new life in Me, a new beginning that ends in eternity with Me. You still get to choose who to worship, who to love, and who to believe. Choose Me, for I am worthy of your worship; I am love, and I am truth. All things wonderful begin with Me.

God

God, I want you to know...

God Wants You to Know...

Smell: to perceive or detect the odor or scent of something or to emit an odor or scent of a specified kind.

To "stop and smell the roses" means more than to take in their scent. Sometimes you just need to stop. Stop thinking, planning, and taking control. Just smell the roses I created for your pleasure.

Take in the sweet, sweet aroma of the Holy Spirit taking control of your life. Let Him do the thinking and planning; you do the doing. Doing My will is easy; doing things your way is hard. You are so busy thinking, planning, and fretting that nothing gets done. Relax, step back, and "smell" the roses.

Are there things you are struggling with? Things I never asked or intended you to do? Stop! Stop doing things your way, and start doing things My way. Start by putting Me first in your life by spending more time with Me, then start praising and honoring Me as Lord God Almighty who was and is and is to come, and finally, love Me with all your heart and your soul and your mind. When you do this, you will emit the sweet aroma of My Spirit.

God

God, I want you to know...

God Wants You to Know...

    Judging: to form, give, or have an opinion; express a bad opinion of someone's behavior often because you think you are better than they are. You have no right to judge other people because of what they look like or what they believe!

    I agree. I made everyone different, all in My image. I love each and every one. People make choices. Whether good or bad, that is between them and Me. You also make choices to do this or that, to say this or that, to believe this or that. That is between you and Me. I will be the judge. If I feel you need reprimanding, I will reprimand you. If I see you going off the path, I will gently lead you back to the path of righteousness. If you don't look the way you should, I can help you with that too. However, I will never condone your judging others, good or bad. You need only to love them. I will take care of judging them. Yes, you can pray for them. Yes, you can bless them, but know that your opinion of them does not matter; only mine does.

    I love you.

Abba Father,
God

God, I want you to know...

God Wants You to Know...

 A wall is a structure or a barrier put in place for protection or privacy. I have built a wall of love around you to protect you from Satan's lies. When you look closely, you will see that the wall is made up of My love, Jesus's salvation, and the Holy Spirit's guidance. Satan cannot penetrate this wall, as long as you maintain it. There are many ways to maintain this wall of love. One would be to love others. Showing My love to others makes you strong and impenetrable. Another would be to give the Holy Spirit complete control of your day. This will protect your wall from collapse and decay. Another would be to say every day, "Jesus loves me, this I know, for the Bible tells me so." Accepting our love grows the wall and allows you to be stronger and stronger every day. I have made this wall up of people who love you. They are there to encourage you, lift you up in prayer, and help you. Let them. A wall can be for privacy, but this wall is transparent. Everyone can see you as you live every day in My love.
 I love you.

God

God, I want you to know...

God Wants You to Know...

Knowledge is a familiarity, awareness, or understanding of someone or something.

To know is to have developed a relationship with someone through meeting and spending time with them.

My Word, the Bible, will give you all the knowledge you will ever need. Read it every day to acquire knowledge. To know Me will require more than just knowledge. You need to have a relationship with Me and spend time with Me to know Me.

I desire to know you. Yes, I have knowledge. I know everything about you, but I desire to know you by spending time with you every day, by meeting you in your secret place, and listening to everything you have to say. They say, "To know Me is to love Me." I say, "To love Me is to know Me." When you love Me as I love you, you will know Me intimately and I you.

Make this a top priority in your life, and all will be well with your soul.

Selah. I love you.

God

God, I want you to know...

God Wants You to Know...

    Come dance with Me. Life is a dance, sometimes a slow dance, sometimes a two-step. Sometimes we dance alone, sometimes in a group. When in a group, listen to the rhythm of that group. Are we all dancing with My Spirit? Are we all singing the same song? If there is any discord or disharmony, leave that group, and join one where I lead the dance. Peace, joy, and love are what we are dancing to. They are the rhythm section. Faith, trust, and obedience are the beat, the unchanging tempo. Can you hear the music? Sway with Me, lean on Me, and let Me lead. Hear the oceans roar and the thunder rumble. Hear the quiet and the stillness. Hear My whisper in your ear, "I love you!"
    Life is a dance. Come dance with Me.
    You will not always feel like dancing, dance anyway. You will feel like leading sometimes. Let Me lead anyway. The success of the dance (your life) is up to you.
    May I have this dance?

God

God, I want you to know...

God Wants You to Know...

Ashes: the remains of something destroyed; ruins.

Do you feel like your life is destroyed, that you are living in the ruins? Does it seem like all you have lived for is as worthless as ashes? Look, I am here to pick you up out of the ashes of sin and despair. I am here to rescue you from Satan's clutches. I am waiting for your cry for help. Sin has destroyed your life, stolen your joy, and left you feeling helpless. I have come to seek and save the lost, to restore all the devil has stolen, to give you a new heart, a new life, and a new reason to live. I am near to the heartbroken, and I save those who are crushed in spirit (contrite in heart, truly sorry for their sin).

Ask me into your heart, and I will come in and give you a new heart, a new life, and a new reason to live. I will never leave you nor forsake you. I will never let you down. I am here for you. Let's do life together.

Love,
God

God, I want you to know...

God Wants You to Know...

Ruin: the disastrous disintegration of someone's life.

Oh, My child, do you not see how Satan is trying to ruin your life? Do you not see that apart from Me, there is no life worth living? I build you up, and Satan tears you down. I give you life, and he gives you death. I offer joy unspeakable, and he entices you with riches and worldly pleasures.

Herein lies the struggle. What do you want? What do you really, really want? Do you want life or death? Do you want joy or a fleeting sense of joy? Do you want to be built up or torn down and left as a pile of ruins? I am the only one who can truly give you the true desires of your heart. I am the only one that truly loves and cares for you. Don't let Satan ruin your life. I have come to restore, rebuild, and rescue you. I ask you again, what do you want? I want you. When you accept Me into your life and give Me complete control, we will be victorious.

God

God, I want you to know...

God Wants You to Know...

Reflection: serious thought or consideration.

This is the time for reflection. This is the time to seriously think about your life and where it is going. It is time for you to consider all your options carefully.

Reflect on your past as you consider your future. Reflect on the good things of your past, the things you need to keep doing, things that you will carry over into your future. Reflect on the bad things, the things you need to stop doing completely, the things that have no place in your future. Reflect on your associations, the people whom you have associated with in the past; will they be in your future? How about me? Will I be in your future? Reflect on your emotions. Were you happy, joyfully at peace in your past? Does your future hold happiness, joy, and peace? Look to me for the answers, look to Me for guidance, and look to Me for the best future you can have.

I love you.

God

God, I want you to know...

God Wants You to Know...

Forgive: stop feeling angry or resentful toward someone for an offense, flaw, or mistake.

Forgive: cancel a debt.

You have been forgiven. I have paid the debt you owe. All your sins have been forgiven; you are as white as snow. Not only have I forgiven the sins of your past but also the ones now and in the future. I remember them no more.

Now it is your turn. Stop feeling angry toward yourself for being imperfect, for being flawed, or for making a mistake. Forgive, forget, and move on. Unforgiveness keeps you captive. I came to set you free.

Forgive those who make you feel angry or flawed. Forgive those who offended you or just made a mistake. Forgive, forget, and move on.

Cancel their debt; they owe you nothing.

Learn to love them and you as I do.

Surrender to Me, and I will show you how.

God

God, I want you to know...

God Wants You to Know...

Heart: the central or innermost part of something.

Without a heart, you are nothing. Without the heart organ, a body cannot live. Without My heart living in you, you are spiritually dead. Your physical heart pumps blood to all parts of your body. Your spiritual heart pumps love to all parts of the body of Christ. Your physical heart can be diseased or not working 100 percent. Your spiritual heart can also be diseased with sin or not working 100 percent because it is not fully committed to Me. Man can replace a diseased heart with a healthy one. I can replace a sinful heart with a new heart, giving you a new life and a new purpose. Give Me your diseased, sinful heart, and I will replace it with My heart, one full of love, joy, and peace.

I want to be the central innermost part of you. I want to give you life—a new life and a life we live together forever.

God

God, I want you to know...

God Wants You to Know...

Barrier: a circumstance or obstacle that keeps people or things apart or prevents communication or progress.

There are many barriers that keep My children apart from Me. The biggest barrier is sin. Sin comes in many forms: disobedience, complacency, self-indulgence, settling for less, and hatred. These are not man-made barriers, and man alone cannot break down these barriers. Only the Holy Spirit can dismantle these barriers so that you can be with Me and I with you, and we will walk and talk in the garden, and our joy will be complete.

With the Holy Spirit's help, you will be able to tear down and replace each one with My love. Replace disobedience with obedience, complacency with being your best, self-indulgence with always putting others first, settling for less with striving for My very best, and hatred for My love, My compassion, and My heart.

The Holy Spirit is ready to help you. Let him.

God

God, I want you to know...

God Wants You to Know...

Green light means go. When you desire to do My will, to go where I send you, and be who I want you to be, I give you a green light. When you desire to give of yourself, your time, and your money to further My Gospel and build My kingdom, I give you a green light. When you desire to do the right thing at the right time, for the right reason, I give you a green light.

Red light means stop. When you desire to not do My will or go where I send you or try to be who I want you to be, I give you a red light. When you refuse to give of yourself, your time, and your money to further My Gospel and build My kingdom, I give you a red light. When you no longer desire to do the right thing at the right time, for the right reasons, I give you a red light. S\top!

Turn around, and come back to Me. Put Me first and foremost, want what I want, and do what I desire, and then I will give you once more the green light.

God

God, I want you to know...

God Wants You to Know...

Tears: as if crying from the heart.

Lift up your head, oh downtrodden soul, lift up your head and be made whole. Why so sad and heartbroken? Put your faith in Me, and you will be set free. Wipe away your tears, and put your trust in Me, for I am trustworthy. I see your crying heart. I feel your pain. I understand what you are going through. Give it all to Me, for My yoke is easy and My burden is light. It is not up to you to do life alone. It is not up to you to find a way to "fix it." It is not up to you to endure the pain one more day. Give it all to Me. I am the Healer, the only One that can take away your pain and give your life purpose. I am the only One that can take away the sadness and give you happiness. Give Me your broken heart full of sadness, pain, and tears, and I will give you My heart full of love, joy, and peace.

God

God, I want you to know...

God Wants You to Know...

Time: the indefinite continued progress of existence and events in the past, present, and future, regarded as a whole.

Time is endless. Like Me, it has no beginning and no end. It is immeasurable, infinite, and progressive. I control the amount of time you have; you control the way you use it. I control the length of time you have here on earth; you control how you live it. You control your time by the decisions you make. I give you choices every day on how to use the time I give you. You can choose to spend it wisely or to waste it. You can choose to spend it with Me or without Me. You can choose to spend the time I give you depressed, anxious, and worried or happy, joyous, and at peace.

Choose Me above all others. Put Me first and foremost in your life, and your time will be well spent. Give Me complete control of your time, and you will be made whole.

God

God, I want you to know...

God Wants You to Know...

"Please leave a message at the sound of the tone, and I will get back to you" is something you will never hear Me say. When you call out to Me, I answer immediately. I am always just a prayer away. I have time for You, My child. Always you can tell Me everything: what's bothering you, what you desire, and what you would like Me to do for you or others. Confide in Me. I am worthy of your trust in Me. Ask in confidence. I will reward your faith in Me. Tell Me everything. Don't leave anything out, for I care for you and I always have time for you. When we talk it out, we will find a solution for your problems, answers to your questions, and I will bless you with the desires of your heart.

I covet your prayers. My time spent with you is the most enjoyable thing I do all day. I hope you can say the same. Don't be a stranger. Call Me anytime.

I love you,
God

God, I want you to know...

God Wants You to Know...

    I am not sorry. I have done nothing wrong. I will make no apologies. Everything I do is for a reason. Everything I say has a purpose. Everything I am is for your good and My glory. I want you to be more like Me in these respects. Strive to do that which is right. Do things on purpose and for a purpose. Do only the things that I ordain. Live your life in such a way that it reflects My love, My peace, and My joy. Speak only the words I give you—the words of truth and life. Give the Holy Spirit complete control of your life every day. Live in the spirit and not the flesh.

    To love, to honor, and to glorify Me is to live life to the fullest and to have no regrets. This is the life I have for you.

    Come, live your life in Me, for Me, and all about Me. You will not regret it, and you will never have to say you are sorry because I have already forgiven you when I redeemed you. Granted, you will never be perfect, but you will always be forgiven.

I love you.
God

God, I want you to know...

God Wants You to Know...

    I want you to know that you are loved, you are worthy, and you are enough. I am not the only one that loves you. Look around; there are many. You are worthy of My love and theirs. I make you worthy. It is by My grace and mine alone. Embrace My grace, as you love others as I love you. You are enough. I make it so. You do not need to strive in your own power to be more than you are. In Me, you are enough. On your own, not so much. Trust and rely on Me, and the victory of every battle you face will be ours.

    They say to fight the good fight. I say, let Me fight your battles. You put on the armor of God and stand and watch your adversaries fall. Ours is the victory—victory in Jesus. No foe can stand against us.

    I love you. I make you worthy, and in Me, you are enough. Amen.

Papa God

God, I want you to know...

God Wants You to Know...

A house is a dwelling place. A home is a place where one lives permanently. I made your body a house for you to live in while you are on earth. I made mansions in heaven to be your home.

This world is not your home. You are just passing through on your way home.

Don't get caught up in all that is going on here; it is temporary. Live for those things that are eternal.

Live for the prize you will get when you win the race and when you live victoriously over sin and death. Jesus died so you can have this victory. When Satan tempts you to give up, hold on to Me with everything you've got. When others tempt you to live the way they do, choose not to listen to them. When you begin to doubt yourself, your dreams, and your goals, lean on Me all the more. There are voices and choices. Listen to Me, and choose to follow Me. I am the only one who will lead you home for all eternity.

God

God, I want you to know...

God Wants You to Know...

My child, I would like to make a point. The point is that I love you! I have loved you before you were in your mother's womb. Even before you were born, I had a plan for your life—a plan for peace and well-being and not for disaster—to give you a future and a hope. I want you to want Me to be your loving Father and to want to be more like Me every day. I desire for you to live our dreams and accomplish our goals together. Where you go, I go. Where you are, there I am also. We are inseparable, and it is My love that binds us together.

Love Me with all your heart, your mind, and your strength, and you will have nothing to fear, for all will be well with your soul.

Yes, I will love you no matter what, but why go there? Stay with Me. Honor and glorify Me at all times, and you will not have to go through the pain and sorrow disobedience brings. Again, I love you!

Father God

God, I want you to know...

God Wants You to Know...

The Trinity—God the Father, God the Son, and God the Holy Spirit—I AM Three in One. I am your Father, Jesus's Father, and the Father of all who believe in Me and accept My Son as Savior. God the Son, We are inseparable; We are the same but have different roles. As the Son, I came to earth to save the world from their sins. As God the Father, it was I who sent Him and gave Him the strength to do all He did, and to go through all that He went through. God the Holy Spirit came later and was sent to dwell in the hearts of those who accept Me as Lord and Savior. My role as Holy Spirit is to comfort and guide My children, to show them right from wrong, to keep them on the narrow path, and to take complete control of their lives when they let Me.

You have access to all three of Us. Come to the Father, come to the Son, and come to the Holy Spirit. We are Three in One.

God

God, I want you to know...

God Wants You to Know...

    You were never meant to know all that I know. I know everything that was, is now, and is to come. That responsibility is mine. So don't worry if you feel like you are in the dark sometimes. Don't get upset if you don't know all there is to know about a situation, and don't panic if something happens that you didn't know anything about. Just knowing that I know should be enough.

    Believe in Me when I say I love you and will not harm you. Have faith in Me to do the right thing at all times, and trust Me to have My best interest for you in mind at all times. Knowing all things puts Me in control, and that is the way it should be.

    I give you knowledge through experience, through life lessons, and through My Word. Listen to what I am telling you, learn by doing, and depend on Me for everything. You don't know what you don't know, and that is the way it will be until I let you know. Trust Me.

God

God, I want you to know...

The pages before this page were given to me personally by God. The pages after this page were given to me for someone else. Most of the recipients have given me permission to include them in this book.

God Wants You to Know...

Written to a pastor who lost his wife to cancer.
God wants you to know:

Welcome back. I have missed you. I have been waiting for you. I am so happy that you are back in My arms where you belong. I know how hard it was for you to lose your wife. I know you needed time to process it and come to grips with the finality of her passing, of never being by her side again here on earth. Cheer up. She is here by My side, and she is more beautiful than you could ever imagine, loving, kind, pain-free, and loving where she is at. Be happy for her.

It is time for you to be happy. It is time for you to have dreams and goals, for you to live out the dreams I give you, and to obtain the goals we set together. Some of these things I have set in motion, others will come as you step out with a leap of faith. You have enough time left to make a difference in many, many lives. Don't waste a minute! Meet with Me every morning, and we will plan our day together. Don't worry about anything. I am your Provider, your Savior, and the Lover of your soul. Do those things I ask you to do, go where I ask you to go, and become the son I am already proud of. I will never leave you nor forsake you. I love you so very much.

Abba Father,
God

God, I want you to know...

God Wants You to Know...

To a missionary to Haiti, Mary Anderson.
Mary, God wants you to know:

I love you! I love you! I love you!

There is nothing that you can do to change that. Nothing! Nothing that you have done, are doing, or will do can change the love I have for you. My love is unconditional, everlasting, and precious. You cannot buy it, earn it, or deserve it. The love I have for you is nothing short of amazing. You are My child, and I love you!

I have many children where I have sent you, and I love them as I love you, like I want you to love them. I know they are not all lovely or for that matter lovable, but I will help you to love them, whatever it takes. I am not asking you to do the impossible. In Me all things are possible. I am not asking you to do this alone, for I am with you always. I am not asking you to find a way, for I am the Way, the Truth, and the Light. I will guide you, protect you, and keep you from harm.

I, however, cannot do this alone. I need you to make the decision, put your faith in Me, and give Me complete control of every situation I put you in.

I love you, Mary. You are right where I want you. Never doubt Me or My love for you.

Your heavenly Father,
God

God, I want you to know...

God Wants You to Know...

Haiti team, God would say to all of you:

Thank you. Thank you for answering My call! Thank you for your willingness to be used by Me in Haiti.

The most important thing I need you to do this week in Haiti is to love each and every one you meet. They don't need your judgment. They don't need your help. They don't need you to fix anything. All they need is love. You love them, and I will do the rest. The reason they do not know their identity is because they don't know how much I love them. They are judged, given help they don't need, made to feel that they are broken and unloved. These are My children. I am their Provider. I am their Helper. I am their Caregiver. I am all they need! Be My ambassadors of love in Haiti this week, and I will bless you and everything you do.

Thank you, thank you, thank you.

Go in love! Go in Me.

I AM Love.

God

God, I want you to know...

God Wants You to Know...

I am so proud of you! You are My son in whom I am well pleased. Every day your thoughts are more and more about Me and the plans I have for you. It has not always been so. Don't look back! Don't go back! Keep going forward! Keep your eyes on Me, always! There is nothing for you in the past, but there is everything for you in your future. How do you get to your future, you ask? By living in the present in My presence. I desire to meet with you every day. Pick a time that works for you. Anytime is fine. I will be waiting for you at that time, every day.

I want you to know that Satan wants you back. He will do everything he knows to get you back! Don't underestimate his power or his sincerity. I love you! I will never let you go. I will never leave you nor forsake you. Don't underestimate My power or My sincerity! We are in a battle. Read the Bible. Satan loses! We, you and I, are victorious!

There are so many others that have been where you have been, so many that I can help. Will you help Me help them? I want you! I can use someone else, but you are My first choice. Be the "hope" for those I will send your way. Do it because you love Me, and I will open doors for you and do for you things beyond your hope or imagination. We are a team that cannot be defeated!

See you tomorrow at our special time.

Your Papa,
God

God, I want you to know...

God Wants You to Know...

You are not alone. There are many people that have the same feelings you are experiencing. What makes you different than the millions in your situation is that you come out victorious!

This is how you are going to win this battle: put your MIND to the task on hand. The task on hand is defeating the enemy! Think of nothing else, day and night. Keep your MIND on Me, and I will show you how to defeat Satan. Remember, he is not only your enemy, but he is My enemy too! I defeated him on the cross. Now it is your turn to defeat him in your life.

Body. Keep your body pure. Your body is My temple. Treat it accordingly! Do only those things that glorify Me.

Soul. That part of you that I came to save, that part of you that will live with Me forever and forever, and that part of you where My love resides. My love is the key to victory. Use this key to open up a whole new way of living—living a life of love!

Spirit. The Holy Spirit! Without the Holy Spirit, there is no hope of victory. He is whom you will depend on to fight the battle for you. He is the One you will get your strength from. When you don't know what to do or how to do it, He will guide you. Give Him full control of your life, and you will be victorious!

I love you very much! I am very proud of you! There is no one else I would rather have as a general in My army! Carry on!

Your Commander in Chief,
God

God, I want you to know...

God Wants You to Know...

My dear child,

I love you so much! I love you more than you love your wife. I love you more than you love your children. I love you more than you love yourself. My love for you is everlasting, ever present, and everything you will ever need. It is because of My love that you have been asked to do what you are doing. It is because of My love that you are in the stage of life you are in. It is because of My love that you are going through what you are going through right now.

I need you to understand that I expect you to love your wife, your kids, and Me with the love I give you—love everlasting, ever present, and all sufficient.

I will always love you. I will always be here for you. I will always take care of you. Go and do likewise to those I have given you, and never give up!

I love you more than you will ever know.

Your heavenly Father,
God (Agape)

PS: I am so proud of you!

God, I want you to know...

God Wants You to Know...

You don't know what you don't know. You don't know what I have planned for you. You don't know the future you are going to experience. You don't know Me as well as you are going to. Be not afraid. I love you and am going to reveal to you those things you don't know; the things I have planned for you, and the future you will live. I love you. Put Me first in your life, and you will be more successful than you can ever imagine. I will never leave you nor forsake you. Don't ever leave Me nor forsake Me. We are a team for now and forever.

Your Papa,
God

God, I want you to know...

God Wants You to Know...

I am so proud to be your Papa! A father couldn't be blessed more than I am. As I watch you grow up in the faith, becoming a mature Christian, becoming more and more dependent on Me every day, every moment, every instant, as you should be, I am so proud.

Oh, I know you are not perfect. None of My children are. Sincerity is so much more important than perfection. Your sincerity, your "stick-to-itiveness," is impressive. Your willingness to obey Me without hesitation is awesome. Your being available to Me both day and night is amazing. You are My child in whom I am well pleased.

Be assured, I know the plans I have for you, plans to prosper you and not to harm you, plans to give you a hope and a future—a future more wonderful than your finite mind can imagine.

I am so excited just thinking about it! Are you ready, My child?

Are you ready for the ride of a lifetime? Are you ready for the plans I have for you?

Continue on as you have been, and you will be prepared for all I have planned for you. Remember, I will never leave nor forsake you. I will never let you down, and never will you let Me down. I know because I am your Papa and I have raised you right. I love you more than you can fathom.

Your Papa,
God

God, I want you to know...

God Wants You to Know...

    Freedom! Freedom! Freedom! In Me there is freedom! Freedom to dance, freedom to sing, and freedom to express your love for Me. There are many ways to express your love for me, ways you haven't thought of yet. You have seen many ways that I express My love to My people, you have seen many ways other people express My love to others, and you have experienced My love in many ways. Now I want these experiences to be a way of life for you.

    I am ready to break the bondages that are preventing you from living this life I came to give you. I am ready, willing, and able to make this a reality in your life. Are you ready? Are you willing? You are able!

    I love you so much! You are so special to Me. I know all the things that you are going through. You need to know that I am with you. I have not forsaken you. I never will!

    I have so much more for you. I have more love, more life, and more freedom! All you have to do is want what I have for you, and I will give it to you. Ask, and you shall receive!

All My love,
Your heavenly Father, God

God, I want you to know...

God Wants You to Know...

    My heart is breaking. I miss you so much! You are My prodigal son. I miss you so much! Come home. It is time to come home. I've been waiting and waiting and waiting. Yes, I will wait forever if that is what it takes, but do you really want to miss out on what I have planned for you now? Every day I have things for you, things I want to give you, things I want you to do for Me, and things I want to do for you.

    Every day I miss you more and more. Every day I love you more and more. Every day I long for you. Come home, come back home, don't wait any longer. Run into My loving arms. I love you so much! Come just the way you are. Don't change a thing.

God

God, I want you to know...

God Wants You to Know...

    I love you. I love you more today than I did yesterday. I love you because I am Love. I love you because that is what I do as a Father; I love My children. I loved you before you were born. I love you now just the way you are, and I love, love, love what the future holds for you. Who you are becoming, the life you will be living, and the dream that will become reality are all for My glory, and I am very excited for you, My child.

    I know you struggle with fear, doubt, and unworthiness, but listen to Me, trust in Me, and lean not on your own understanding and insight, and the fear will disappear. Know that I am God, and all doubt will be gone. You are My child, the child of the Most High God, and that makes you worthy.

    I know you have lots of questions. Ask Me. I have all the answers. I know you worry if it is My will or not. My will for you is to trust and obey. If you do that, you will be in My will, and your life will flourish.

    The first step is the hardest. Just take it with a leap of faith, and you will be called a mountain mover. The second step is a step of love. You take it because you love Me. Step-by-step we are walking the road of life I have prepared for you, you and Me, side by side, the way I have always dreamed it would be.

    Do you trust me? I know you love Me, but do you trust me? Do you know in your heart of hearts that I will never leave you nor forsake you, that nothing you do or don't do, you say or don't say will ever stop Me from loving you? You can trust Me.

Abba Father,
God

God, I want you to know...

God Wants You to Know...

Sons and daughters, honor your fathers as I honor My Father in heaven. I have given you the father I wanted you to have. Is he perfect? Did he always obey me? Could I have picked someone better? Don't ask! Trust me! I know what I am doing. I know what you need. I know the reasons things happen and why other things don't.

Sons and daughters, love your father as I love My father in heaven. Love him no matter what. Love him when he is loving. Love him when you think he isn't. Your love will make all the difference in your relationship with your earthly dad and your heavenly Father.

Sons and daughters, trust Me. Your father loves you very much, and so do I.

Abba Father,
God

God, I want you to know...

God Wants You to Know...

    This is a new day! I want to show you a new way—a new way to live for Me and a new way to do those everyday things that make up your life. Behold, old things have passed away, all things are new. Leave the old, embrace the new!

    I love you! I love everything about you! I made you just the way you are for a purpose—my purpose. I will never leave you nor forsake you. I want you in My life as much as you need Me in yours.

    I know you. I know everything about you. I know your every thought. I know your future and your past. If you have any questions, please ask.

    My child, this is a new day, and I am so excited to live this and every day with you.

    I love you more than you will ever know.

Your all-knowing Father,
God

God, I want you to know...

God Wants You to Know...

My dear child,

    I love you! I love you! I love you!
    I have always loved you, but I love you more now than ever before. Words can't express the love I have for you. Feelings can't express the love I have for you. Blessings can't express the love I have for you.
    I can tell you I love you. I can make you feel My love. I can bless you above and beyond anything you can imagine, but if you don't love Me back, what good is it?
    Do you love me? I desire for you to tell Me you love Me every day. I desire for you to make Me feel the love you have for Me every day. I desire for you to bless Me as I have blessed you every day. This is the desire of My heart for you.
    I love you! I love you! I love you! Do you love me? I desire your love above and beyond all things.
    You are My child and I love you.

Your Father,
God

God, I want you to know...

God Wants You to Know...

To the dozen college kids that were picked up on Easter Sunday morning for church in my seven-passenger van.
God wants you to know:

Wow! You guys are amazing! I love that going to church is so important to you! I love your attitude that nothing can hinder you from celebrating My resurrection. I love that you love Me.

I am alive! Hallelujah! I am alive in the hearts of those who love Me and have accepted Me into their hearts. I am alive in every situation you invite Me into in your lives. I am alive so you can live in Me all the days of your life.

My children, I love you very much!

Love, your Father,
God

P.S. See you next Sunday!

God, I want you to know...

God Wants You to Know...

My dear child,

I love you so much! I don't think you understand. I LOVE YOU just the way you are! There is nothing you can do to make Me love you any less or any more. My LOVE is unconditional. You can't earn it. You cannot escape it. My love knows no end. My love goes on and on and on, forever!

Please stop rejecting Me. Please stop finding excuses to stay the way you are. I have so much more for you.

The past is just that: the past. The future is yet to come. Let's do your future together.

I have provided you with friends and family to help you on our journey, the journey you and I are on together. I can't promise you that it will be easy, but I can promise you that I will not forsake you nor leave you stranded. You cannot do this alone, and I would never, never ask you to.

I love you so much!

I will wait until you are ready, but you must decide to do this. You must decide to not listen to those on the right who would say to you, "You do not need to do this now. Wait until you feel more worthy" or those on the left that would say to you, "Look inward, be strong, and you can do this by yourself, in your own power." That is the father of lies trying to keep you for his own. Don't listen to him! Don't be persuaded by the lies of Satan.

Listen to me! I am calling you! I am calling you to do great and mighty things!

I am so excited! We can do this!

God

God, I want you to know...

God Wants You to Know...

God is saying to you:

Trust in Me. My wisdom is yours for the asking. Turn to Me when you don't understand. Turn to Me when you are confused. Turn to Me when things don't seem to make sense. I alone have the answers to all your questions. I alone know what you need to know and when you need to know it.

Like the farmer, I will show you what to do next and how to do it in each and every situation. First, you prepare the soil—your heart—by reading your Bible and spending time with Me, but that alone is not enough. Seeds need to be planted, proper seeds in proper places and in proper ways. I will teach you in a way you will understand, for I am the Lord of heaven's armies and I am a wonderful Teacher.

I will teach you what it means to use a light stick rather than a heavy sledge and beating lightly with a flail and never a threshing wheel and to stop pounding the grain when it is crushed and to never pulverize it.

I will teach you these things so that you can reap a harvest of wonderful fruit in your life.

I will plant in you the fruits of My spirit: love, peace, joy, patience, kindness, goodness, faithfulness, gentleness, and self-control. I will plant these in your heart and soul, and you will water them with faith, trust, and obedience.

Now go and do the things I am teaching you so that someday, very soon, you will be able to teach others to do the same.

I love you, My daughter, and I am very proud of you.

Your Abba Father,
God

PS: Trust me! I am with you always, and I will never forsake you nor leave you unequipped to do My will.

God, I want you to know...

God Wants You to Know...

To a man in Baton Rouge at the time of the flooding. God would say to you:

I am so proud of you! I love you very much! I know the challenges you have just gone through. I know how difficult it has been. After all you have gone through, you give Me praise. After all the losses you have experienced, you still bless others. After all the suffering, you still count your blessings.

I am so proud of you! You love Me very, very much, and it shows! Remember, it is the small things that make the difference. Trust in Me, and together, you and I will make a difference in the lives of many.

Thank you for all you have done for Me. Now let Me do even more for you. I want to bless you beyond measure. I want to give you peace that passeth all understanding and joy unspeakable, full of glory!

I have all of this and so much more in store for you in the days ahead. I am with you. I will never leave you nor forsake you, no matter what!

I love you, son.

Papa God

PS: I am so excited about what I have planned for you in the days ahead!

God, I want you to know...

God Wants You to Know...

    I made you to be an encourager. Your job is to encourage everyone you meet. Your job is to make others feel good about themselves. Your job is to show the love of Jesus to everyone you meet. I want you to know that you are doing an excellent job! I am very proud of you! I could not have picked a better person to do this job.

    I know that at times you need to be encouraged. I know that it is not always easy to be the one giving, giving, and giving. Do not fear. I am with you always! I am your Provider. I will provide you with love, heavenly knowledge, strength, and encouragement. Come to Me when you are heavy-laden and discouraged. I will never let you down!

    I love you! I love you more than you can ever imagine!

    The love I love you with is the love you give away every day. The more you give away, the more I give you. You will never run out. There is always more where that came from.

    Now go in peace—the peace that passeth all understanding. Go in love—the love that never fails. Go in My name—the name that is above all others.

With all My love,
Papa God

PS: Always praise God from whom all blessings flow!

God, I want you to know...

11/25/22

Mary Jane,
 God wants you to know...
that you very precious
to Him and He loves you
very much.
 May these writings bless
you as you spend time
with God.
   — Ruth L. Coffing